Beautiful Wheel

Beautiful Wheel

Theodore Deppe

ARLEN HOUSE

Beautiful Wheel

is published in 2014 by
ARLEN HOUSE
42 Grange Abbey Road
Baldoyle
Dublin 13
Ireland
Phone/Fax: 353 86 8207617
Email: arlenhouse@gmail.com
www.arlenhouse.blogspot.com

978–1–85132–084–4, paperback

Distributed internationally by
SYRACUSE UNIVERSITY PRESS
621 Skytop Road, Suite 110
Syracuse, NY 13244–5290
Phone: 315–443–5534/Fax: 315–443–5545
Email: supress@syr.edu

Typesetting ¦ Arlen House
Artwork ¦ 'Bela Rada' by Caitlin Deppe
Photography by Benjamin Lewando

CONTENTS

ACKNOWLEDGMENTS

The author wishes to thank the editors of the following journals where these poems appeared, often in earlier versions:

Arsenic Lobster, Cyphers, Green Mountains Review, New England Review, Poetry Ireland Review, Prairie Schooner, Sojourners, Southword, Stinging Fly, Solstice Online, The New Guard, The SHOp, and *Theodate.*

I'd like to thank Betsy Sholl, Kate Newmann, and Joan Newmann, who read these poems and offered so many valuable suggestions. Thanks, too, to Annie Deppe, the first reader of these poems and the joy of my life.

'Shouting at the Window of the Night' from this collection was highly commended by the judges of the Forward Prizes for Poetry and published in *The Forward Book of Poetry 2015.*

For Annie

and in memory of my parents

Alice Minot Deppe and Theodore Robert Deppe

Beautiful Wheel

Inexplicable World

A first set of headphones, purchased
on impulse in an airport, then tried
at home while paying bills, but alone

with the music
I sing along or drum with my hands,
making enough noise

that my wife can hear it in her study.
I've tried guarding
myself, keeping the music within,

but this morning I'm humming again
as Pablo Casals plays
Manuel de Falla's 'Nana',

a complication since Casals also
hums, or groans, or growls as he plays,
a low whale song that sometimes precedes

the bow then merges with it.
When I come forth from my sound-thicket
I find Annie singing

in the kitchen, cleaning up
the mess I made cooking our breakfast.
How often she whistles

as she writes, or hums
without knowing it as she shops,
an endearing

habit her mother once had.
Listening to her after Casals,
it seems the whole

inexplicable
world might have come about
through someone's humming to herself.

She slips from one song
to the next, none of it anything I know,
and listening from the door

I could be at the dawn of creation,
hearing the music that is behind,
or before, or inside everything,

unguarded self-song
moving above the dishes,
bringing order to the cups and bowls.

Bela Rada

1

During my youth, on a thousand-mile walk
around Ireland, my dreams grew strange
and bright as planets, and I woke once,
laughing, having witnessed my own birth:

a young woman, holding her newborn, stepped
from rows of tasseling corn as a voice-over
intoned, *And they named him Bela Rada.*
Bela, Beautiful, *Rada,* Wheel: that's how I

translated it, recalling a Serbian circle dance
I'd known in college, though later I found it meant
Beautiful Rada – Rada is a woman's name.
No matter, she's part of me now: *Bela Rada.*

2

This morning, our second in Languedoc, I woke
repeating *Belarus*. In daylight, I know it means
White Russia, but the sun's logic isn't night's.
In my dream it was *Bela*, Beautiful, *Rus*, Russian.

A friend had phoned from Spokane – *Are you awake,*
she asked, *or are you still dreaming*? She
was at a wedding where things were going
terribly wrong – the body of a waitress from Belarus

(or did she say Beltane?) was discovered
in a ballroom. Then I was in Spokane myself,
stepping over yellow tape, assuring the groom,
This is not a sign. Don't call off the marriage.

3

In Spokane the only place with a proper
dream ballroom is the Davenport, the same hotel
where Vachel Lindsay once lived. Epileptic,
prone to visions, Lindsay styled himself the last

of the troubadours and set off to preach the gospel
of beauty. Today, some of his work strikes me
as tedious, but when I was nineteen his *Handy Guide*
for Beggars inspired my six-month walk.

I liked, too, that Lindsay, while recovering
at the Davenport from a breakdown, met a woman
half his age, and beautiful. They married the next day
in what he called *a wedding by spontaneous combustion.*

4

The gospel of beauty. Perhaps it began here
in Languedoc in songs composed by troubadours
for the Cathar women of Cabaret? Though the church
saw them as heretics, their beauty called forth

the praise of poets like Vidal and de Miraval.
Yesterday, we climbed to their ruined chateaux,
negotiating the same paths once taken
by a hundred Cathars from the village of Bram –

blinded by Crusaders, noses and upper lips cut off,
they were sent by the church as a warning
to the citizens of Cabaret. Passion and beauty
and sorrow, all raised under one roof.

5

A few weeks after they met, my parents wed –
spontaneous combustion, yes, but also the war meant
there wasn't time to take things slowly.
They were in Idaho, not far from Spokane,

living in a motel suite with my father's best man
and his new bride. And when, on a training flight,
his friend crashed into a mountain, my father
could only watch from his own plane and keep flying.

That night, his friend's lovely wife clawed
my father's face. Dostoyevsky said, *Beauty*
will save the world, but when has beauty
ever saved anything, even itself?

6

And where did Lindsay's gospel of beauty lead him?
He drank a bottle of Lysol in the same house
where he was born. A man flies into a mountainside.
A girl from Belarus is found

in the Marie Antoinette ballroom with its accents
of 22-carat gold. The church spares one man's eyes
so he can lead the other Cathars up the cypress-lined
precipice as an example for *wrong-believers*.

And Dostoyevsky's Prince Myshkin?
Having proclaimed that beauty would save the world,
this gentle visionary fell in love with two
magnificent women at once and of course went mad.

7

In *The Maltese Falcon,* a man named Flitcraft
was almost killed by a falling beam.
Understanding then that life is random, he vanished,
then showed up at the Davenport

with a new wife much like his first.
Sam Spade liked that Flitcraft *adjusted himself*
to beams falling, and then no more of them fell,
and he adjusted himself to them not falling.

Hard to tell sometimes if the Davenport
is a hotel in a novel, or in real life, or in a dream.
So many beautiful people check in and disappear:
Clark Gable, Sarah Bernhardt, Amelia Earhart.

8

And those who have managed thus far
not to disappear? Spontaneous combustion –
strange the people it joins. My parents
outgrew first love, then found love

again and again, together.
Sixty-three years since beauty drew them close,
and they must help each other now
with the simplest chores. Blindness, surgeries,

depression, and all the rest, yet sometimes
when they look at each other,
they seem to realize how lucky they are.
Love and loss and love again. *Bela Rada*.

9

Our last full day in Languedoc, we visit two more
Cathar strongholds, hilltop castles that couldn't
stave off Crusaders or Inquisitors. Still, against
all evidence, I want to believe Dostoyevsky

about beauty. The owls call out as we fall asleep,
and come morning a dream in which I'm toasting
a bride and groom in an orchard, only it's not me,
I seem to be the girl from Belarus, disfigured

and somehow beautiful, wishing them luck. Belarus,
or *Bela Rada,* the whirl of spokes. We breakfast
on the terrace in dawn's birthlight, while everything
plunges in hazy green into the ridge-shadowed ravine.

La Vie de la Valise

It's time, his wife says, to tally up
the transatlantic flights – two hundred thousand
miles! Almost enough to reach the moon,
but would there be enough sky miles left
to get back home? And where would that be?
Each year, they unpack somewhere new,
and it's wonderful, the places
they've been privileged to live,
but at a party's end a friend wishes them
safe home, and his wife almost weeps.

He wakes, sees lights below, asks, Newfoundland
already? She says, gently, you're always
somewhere above Newfoundland. These days,
haunted by a child in a film who sings in a railway car,
they wish each other *Latcho Drom*, safe journey.
An unplanned month before the next move,
so they cross the skies to Languedoc,
land of troubadours and heretics, stay
in a house of artists where everyone's on the move,
everyone's carrying their own spiritual valise.

And here, for a while, the earth
is under their feet, they follow a river's gleam
to a remote orchard, then head back at dusk.
Which is how, emerging from twilight trees
as, one by one, lights come on
in the shining village above them,
they hear the antiphonal calls of owls
from both hills, safe home, safe journey,
safe home, safe journey, or whatever it is
that birds of prey cry out on a summer's night.

The Place of the Green Wand

Something called a GiveBox appeared
this fall on Falckensteinstraße, and my first gift

was a memory: Dorothy Day, decades ago,
gently quoting Saint Basil to me: *If you have*

two coats, you've stolen one from the poor.
Like a walk-in cupboard on the sidewalk, brightly

painted, decked out with flowers, this GiveBox
is for the anonymous exchange of gifts.

I brought books here and found a biography
of Tolstoy, who once made my teenaged self

dream of giving away everything, and now,
over a whiskey, the idea returns: what if

I stripped myself of all but the necessary,
left things off, day by day, at the GiveBox?

Of course, whatever his genius, Tolstoy's life
ended in confusion, in quarrels, in flight –

did he really think, at 82, he could dispossess
himself and set off wandering? When his body

was brought home, it was buried
in the place of the green wand,

the glade where his twelve-year-old brother
once told a story about a stick

hidden in the earth that, if found, would bring
lasting happiness to us all.

As though, having all but rejected his own novels,
Tolstoy could dispense with everything

but story – he wanted no tombstone,
no service, no clergy, and after all he had written

it was the legend his brother made up
that he turned to. A parable Dorothy Day,

who lived to 83, took seriously until the end.
I met her in my teens when she was in her 70s,

just out of jail after picketing for the rights
of migrants. Visiting a nephew

who was dating my sister, she joined us
for dinner – someday, someone may ask me

the old question, *If you could have a meal*
with anyone, living or dead ...

Going to a French restaurant
with Dorothy Day would be a good answer,

and I was lucky enough to actually do it,
only I wasn't allowed in the restaurant.

Because I'd read Gandhi, who of course
had read Tolstoy, I was trying not to buy leather

and wore a rope belt, and canvas shoes.
And Dorothy, who had reason enough

to scoff at those who called her a saint,
rose to the height of a prophet

and let the restaurant know she expected
so much more of them than their dress code.

In an Italian restaurant down the block
she introduced me to *bruschetta al pomodoro,*

then spoke of so many things
I wish I could begin to recall now.

What was it that boy in his canvas shoes
was searching for?

Is there still time to set off at last
for the place of the green wand?

Shouting at the Windows of the Night
2 November 1965

My *birthday of the electric guitar.* It might for me
have been nothing more than the four of us
practising in the basement, *Louie Louie*

because our governor tried to ban the song statewide,
thereby proclaiming it *the* anthem any Indiana band
must learn first. Johnny claimed

he knew the real version, lyrics so lewd
the Kingsmen had to slur them, so we mastered the art
of mumbling the words meaningfully.

Then someone said we'd never beat the government
in making the obscene unclear,
so in that not-quite soundproof cellar –

until Father came down to say, *Boys,*
it's a school night – we shouted the wrong words
to *Louie Louie* as clearly as we could.

I didn't hear the news until later, but the same day
I turned fifteen a Quaker from Baltimore
drove through rush-hour red to the Pentagon.

Witnesses disagreed whether Norman Morrison
doused himself in kerosene before or after
he let his infant daughter go, but she was there

as her father became a twelve-foot pillar of fire
roaring at the window of the Defense Secretary.
And no one – not the bystanders, not the police

who rushed to his side,
not Secretary McNamara himself –
no one could make out his last words.

Forty-four birthdays ago, but sometimes
Norman Morrison still draws near
as I celebrate. He who had done

everything he knew how to do – protested, prayed,
refused war taxes – now shares with me
the second of November, the Day of the Dead.

Something in me thinks I understand
giving one's life for others, but what if he meant
to take his daughter with him, what if he thought

an American child must burn
so we would see what napalm does?
The flames rose and at some point this father

let his daughter go. Perhaps he held her
until his arm muscles contracted in a jolt of flame,
or maybe an angel commanded, *Release her,*

though I hope he'd already put her down,
before lighting the match, knowing
this death was his alone.

Witnesses could tell us nothing. They only agreed
they couldn't understand a single word
he shouted at the windows of the night.

One Way She Appeared to Him

She didn't, of course, start the fire,
though he thought she'd set the whole Music School
ablaze – the orange sky puckered
and creased above it, and he couldn't pedal
fast enough to get there.

Earlier that week he'd stepped into a practice hall
and seen her at the dress rehearsal of Ravel's
Piano Concerto for the Left Hand. He was lucky,
he'd been kicked out of high school English
and creative writing classes,

so afternoons he took courses at the university,
and arriving early he'd watched as her fingers
bi-located on the keyboard and the whole orchestra
rose above her like a storm cloud.
No sign of her at the scene of the crime

and it turned out to be just a single practice hall,
a disappointment maybe, though he revelled
at the thought of all those scales and finger positions
roaring into the night – who needs analysis and rote?
Then he realized how many instruments

were in there, every piece of the orchestra
igniting, and maybe he just imagined this,
or maybe he could hear heat pluck the cello strings,
hear flames sear a tightened drum skin,
hear the chords a piano makes as the floor opens

and it falls, and strings, brass and winds follow.
He rode back through a maze of glowing streets,
but once home, where none of the windows
reflected fire, he suddenly felt lost: this boy,
who couldn't read music, wanted to play Ravel,

wanted to perform on the piano he'd heard plunge
through the burning floor, wanted a cadenza
of flame, the pulse and flare of the impossible:
the piano resounded through the trap door
of embers, and everything else followed.

Narrow Road

At seventeen, after reading *Narrow Road*
to the Deep North, I enrolled in Japanese class,

planning to retrace Basho's walk.
Failing to learn his language, I re-imagined

my journey, hiked instead a circle around Ireland,
though Basho came with me as guide.

I got off the Rosslare ferry, reciting
his lines: *With a bit of madness in me*

which is poetry, I plod along like Chikusai
among the wails of the wind.

~

Forty years later, living in Galway now, I dream
I trek into a village where I'm met

by dancers in Japanese costumes. Music
of pipes and drums, multicoloured fans

that flutter like wings, as sparrow dancers
fly around me. My dream-self lifts

two or three feet above the street and realizes,
This is a gift. This is the journey I didn't make.

~

For decades I've looked for a poem
Issa may have written, though maybe

bicycling no-handed to Japanese class
I wrote it myself. If somehow I am

the author, it must be my finest poem:

Sing and fly, sing and fly,
all day long – so much to do,
the busy little sparrows.

Last night, searching the internet
for the elusive poem, I found

Issa's name hidden in *Missa Solemnis,*
Renaissance and *croissant.*

~

After a week of writing about Japan, I wake
to news of a 9-point earthquake near Sendai.
I try to reach friends in Donegal
whose daughter is in Japan, then wonder
if they've already left to visit her.

~

Basho wrote, *We crossed the river Natori*
and went into Sendai. It was the day
when people hang blue irises beneath the eaves.

On television, a 13-foot wave of water, mud,
and burning buildings engulfs Sendai's airport.
Faced with the loss of so many,

it doesn't matter that the road Basho walked
in new sandals with iris-blue straps
has vanished.

~

An explosion in a nuclear reactor in Fukushima
and four trains are missing.

And devastation in Matsushima, a place
Basho called the most beautiful in Japan.

Trying to describe those 260 tiny islands,
some crowned with a single pine, he wrote:

Matsushima, ah!
A-ah, Matsushima, ah!
Matsushima, ah!

~

While the situation in Fukushima grows worse,
we travel to St-Rémy-de-Provence to celebrate
a birthday, visit the hospital where for over a year
Van Gogh lived. At the entrance, irises,
and a traffic mirror where a sparrow

keeps flinging itself at a reflected sparrow.
The only other tourists at the hospital
are Japanese. Usually so animated,
today everyone appears
half-here, half-ten-thousand-miles-away.

~

In the hospital garden, even the blossoming
almond tree with its white impasto petals
against a vivid blue sky seems both itself and
a memory of a tree painted here once.

Beyond these flowering branches, out of sight,
grief beyond measure.
Back at the hotel, looking again for Issa's
busy little sparrows, I find instead:

Beginning of spring –
sparrows at the gate
with their little faces.

~

Woke knowing this should be written in sixes,
for 6 August, or threes, for the Trinity test site,
and rising to find a pen, startled my wife. I said

I'll be right back up, which sounded disoriented,
since we were on the ground floor. *Don't worry,*
I told her, though I was thinking of the world's end.

~

A five-minute Internet clip, filmed by a student
who'd reached safety on a hill, the tsunami
entering Nakatsugawa City. Crowds

are still down there, fleeing for the wooded slopes
as the torrent surges towards them.
Constant shouts. Figures running ahead,

but one person goes back towards
those who are delayed. You don't need
to know Japanese to understand.

~

I've phoned our friends, who were indeed
in Tokyo when the quake hit. The subway
closed, so they walked the crowded, snowy streets

toward their hotel, and when they stopped
to rest, an elderly shopkeeper offered his coat
to their daughter and her five-week-old child.

In Galway, these sparrows. Their little faces.
In Japan, whole towns are gone,
and a second, maybe a third reactor is on fire.

The Lost Notebook

1

Fair enough, we brought them
to the Rodin Museum
to visit the *Gates of Hell*, so they

invited us to the catacombs,
a place we'd never thought of touring,
but who better to lead us

past the sign proclaiming, *Stop,*
You are Entering the Empire
of Death! than our grown children?

2

Almost alone among the six million
anonymous dead, the quarryman
Francois Décure is remembered,

and not for how he performed his day job,
or how he cared for his wife
or any offspring he may have had,

but for what he did in the mines
on his lunch breaks,
which was to chip away at memory

and carve a limestone tableau
of a Minorcan fortress, recreating the view
from his former prison window:

parapets and towers, bridges, stairs
and ramparts still bloom like a night garden
beneath the streets of Paris.

3

Soldier, prisoner, quarryman –
almost nothing in his life resembles mine,
except for all those lunch breaks

I took on night shift decades ago,
climbing out a fourth floor window
onto the slanting hospital roof

where I could perch against a gable
and write. All that summer
I filled a notebook – nighthawks

harrowed the air, the Cumberlands
slept uneasily in the east,
my wife and children

in the apartment across the road
floated above their beds,
and beneath me

in the hospital, someone
was setting off to the realm
of the dead, someone else

was arriving amidst obscenities
and pleas, and having only
a half hour each night,

I scribbled as fast as I could,
I tried to get everything down.
And failed, of course,

and then lost even that –
as my wife's granny said
Three moves are as good as a fire.

I have only the memory of opening
a window and stooping through,
of walking the heights

to my favourite spot, then starting to write
as silent hospital shoes
braced me against the slope of night.

Elegy with a Stopped Knife in It

in memory of Larry Levis

The angel of the Lord grasps Abraham's
huge hand, and the halted knife glistens

inches from Isaac's throat. The naked boy's
contorted mouth would scream if it could

as his father's left hand pins him to the rock:
sunlight and shadow, this world and the next,

everything balanced a split second from the edge.
The model Caravaggio used for Isaac

doubled as the angel, also naked, so Abraham,
stopped in his deed, glares at his offspring's

mirror image. Half vision, half nightmare,
I'm reminded of the dream journal

I kept in college, of entries in which my father –
an absurdly gentle man – strangles me, or else

I'm trying to kill him, then sleep
with my friend's mother. Fathers and sons –

maybe I'd read too much Dostoyevsky,
but I stopped recording dreams, having learned,

I thought, enough. In his poem 'Winter Stars',
Larry Levis's father breaks a farmworker's hand

on a tractor to stop the man from killing
his own father. The knife dazzles and briefly

stops time, and it doesn't matter that in real life
the poet's father broke up a fight between two

young men – Levis needed this attempted parricide
as he made up, as honestly as he could,

a sort of afterlife for his dying father.
Today, in the Uffizi, between glinting blade

and throat, this poet I never met is present.
Abraham's thick left thumb immobilizes

the boy. The son is naked, and the angel.
The bearded father wears a golden robe, red sash

flowing from his waist. So what
if the farm workers were both young men?

The battle is always between father and son.
Say that an angel caused Abraham

and all his descendents to struggle with those
who gave us life and those we helped

bring into this world – the knife
gleams in dreamtime light.

The angel of the Lord also commands us to stop.

String Quartet in C Sharp Minor

for Jean Valentine

Shelves of bottles and tins in faded colours
line the walls – it seems
you're giving a reading in a spirit grocery.
The shop is small and something wild

and wintry at the window
makes it hard to hear, so, as if noticing
we can't follow, you read a piece
without words. A roar goes up the chimney –

now, along with the sleet or snow,
glowing sparks flail at the panes,
and you're singing four parts at once,
something like a late Beethoven quartet,

and it's not true music can't mean
anything –
Astonishing! the cello voice says,
We all see others die

yet none of us believe we ourselves will die.
Until tonight, I wasn't sure I had a soul,
and now you are singing to it, now
you are letting it know it's ok to be mortal.

Eine Kleine (Degenerate) *Nachtmusik*

A professor is someone who talks
in someone else's sleep
– W.H. Auden

Buy a ticket from a Xeroxed soul, glide
over the Oberbaumbrücke, listen as a Polish busker
sings a keepsake from a vanished world.

New to Berlin, each night this spring I've recited
the stations of our U-Bahn line,
recalling and then trying to pronounce each name –

Warschauer Straße, Schlesisches Tor,
Görlitzer Bahnhof – until I follow
that golden train into a dream.

Usually by Kottbusser Tor or Prinzenstraße
the auto-hypnotic wheels take me under.
Hallesches Tor …? Skateboarders

disappear past underground florists.
Such bright shades in the dark,
does bell heather blossom even in Hades?

~

A woman with hair dyed the colour of heather
boards the train, sings a bluesy version
of 'Summertime', then leaves with a few coins.

I'm learning to give to anyone who asks.
Overhead signs announce which dream arrives
in how many minutes on which platform.

Is this the station where I let go
of tomorrow's lesson plans? How else
sleep? Through the windows at Möckernbrücke,

I watch security guards materialize
to question two Turkish musicians who abruptly run.
The train leaves with no ending to their story.

~

Get out in Gleisdreieck, listen on the almost
empty platform to a man play harmonica
very softly, and between song fragments

he speaks earnestly to the space above the tracks.
When I approach with spare change he says,
Didn't you understand, I said this playing

was my gift to all of you. He turns away
to play again, small phrases with a certain broken
beauty, then murmurs a few words to the urban night,

and no, I can't say I understand anything,
but board the train, head to Kurfürstenstraße,
is that next? Or Nollendorfplatz ...?

~

On good nights I start in Warschauer Straße,
pronounce the name, watch gulls soar
above the Spree, so far inland. Struggling

with the sounds of Schlesisches Tor, the mind
clouds over. This time, though, I've made it
to Wittenbergplatz, and signs

that once gave train schedules
warn instead of dangerous unattended parcels.
Now I'm in a church on Kurfürstendamm,

where angry voices outside
shout during a Bach cantata – after weeks
of reports of *increased whispers* and *concrete threats*,

I imagine a hostage situation,
but then the chorus stands
and we seem to rise out of danger's reach.

~

Tonight, after staying up late with a student's thesis,
I make my way down the rosary of stations
and reach the last stop, Uhlandstraße –

Diese Zug endet hier – and I'm in a Berlin
without graffiti, where last week a dance troupe
partially unrobed and inched into a showcase,

seeking footholds on thighs and shoulders, rising
any way they could until, like figures in Rodin's
Gates of Hell, they almost flew.

The performance ended with an accordion
and then a narrow pit: a man and a woman stood,
fought, lay back down

as the next pair rose and found each other, lingered
in a kiss, but the pity is, even when we get it right
we have to lie back down anyway.

~

Still not asleep so I start to name the stations
backwards, Uhlandstraße to Kurfürstendam to –
what's next? Mother of Memory,

come down to the underground, *mind the gap,*
play a little night music, I'll listen and give
whatever I have left. After Kurfürstendam,

Wittenbergplatz? And suddenly I recall,
Wittenberg was the last name
of the first girl I ever kissed.

I'd gladly linger in that memory
– Sherry Wittenberg, in Chicago –
but something leads me through the station

to a plaque listing the *Orte des Schreckens,*
the Places of Terror, and to wake me, Memory
insists I read each name – there are twelve –

though now I recall only Auschwitz, Treblinka,
Buchenwald, Flossenbürg, Dachau, Ravensbrück,
Bergen-Belsen. No use lulling myself

with the list of stations now,
and even if I slept I would be transported
to the realm of *Alptraum,* of nightmare,

so, trying not to disturb my wife, I go
to the next room, start to answer emails
from students, then put on headphones

to listen to Erwin Schulhoff, whose *Duo*
for Violin and Cello I heard for the first time
yesterday. Banned by the Nazis as *degenerate,*

nearly forgotten, his work – dancehall music
for shades, eerie and irresistible – is being
resurrected by the Berlin Philharmonic.

After the occupation, he played jazz
under an assumed name in a piano bar in Prague
until he was discovered and put on a train

to the camp in Würzburg. Forget sleep,
dreaming isn't a poem's purpose,
let the waking world glide and kick a bit

the way Schulhoff makes it do
in this gypsy-tinged piece
penned while Central Europe and History

played their high-stakes duet.
Listen next to *Five Picturesques,*
whose middle movement, *In Futurum,*

consists entirely of rest notes. It's begun to flurry,
Falckensteinstraße accepts
whatever loose change the sky can find,

and for almost two minutes
I listen to the agitated sound of
nothing. Decades before Cage, Schulhoff

crammed this movement with prolonged
feverish runs of demisemiquaver rests
that collide with other intricate notations

for noiselessness. How best
to follow his directions? The whole silent piece
should be played *with feeling*.

THE MONTH OF THE TWO MAPS

For Eva Bourke, whose 'Berlin Notebook' *includes the lines:*
... and the time will come
when all we will have to lose is the world.

1

The Ebstorf Mappa Mundi

Snapshot from 1 March 2009: two open suitcases
beneath a poster of a large, round, 13th century
map of the earth. At the centre
of that vanished world, Christ, rising
from his tomb. To the east, cut off by mountains,
the Garden of Eden. And in the photo's foreground,
folded clothes in travelling bags.
Now that our hosts have left, the flat is ours
for the month of March, and rain falls
on Falckensteinstraße, there is a pizzicato note
to the drops as they bounce off tall panes.
We unpack in the midst of song.

~

In the world of this poem it is March, which means
I can call my mother in far-off Indiana
and have her ask me again *Berlin? But why Berlin?*
One answer is today's concert in the Philharmonie
of *A Soldier's Tale,* then reminding Mother
how she once played Stravinsky
so I could dance for her and leap off walls,
always trying to make it to the waiting chair
before the devil appeared. It is March,
which means each day Mother is walking
a little farther. No one knows
that in her brain the cancer's unpacking.

~

Indiana isn't on this world map,
but as Melville says, *True places never are*.
If the cartographer had dreamed of it
he would have placed Indiana
in the heavenly island Saint Brendan found
on his voyage west. He might have drawn
dragons marching down some path
in the burning corn, might have depicted
strange, many-winged people. Even the largest
map of the world can't include everything:
someone decides which rivers and countries
are important, and which cities, which peoples extra.

~

I had to be in the green stuffed chair before the devil
appeared and Stravinsky's narrator said,
You must choose between things. One happy thing
is all happy things. Two things, it's as if
they never were. Such a strange story to dance out.
Such enthusiasm in my one-woman audience.
Hearing *A Soldier's Tale* performed in Berlin,
I'm in Indiana again, and all things seem possible,
the cancer isn't on any map yet, and as long as I stay
in the world of the poem, within its walls,
All shall be well, and all shall be well,
and all manner of things shall be well.

~

The original map, drawn painstakingly
by Gervase of Tilbury, was destroyed
by Operation Gomorrah when Hamburg was razed
in 1943. The bombs caused a wall of flame

that could outrace any living thing, a mammoth
fire tornado that thundered through the city
ending, in minutes, 40,000 lives. Even
the asphalt streets caught fire. A photograph
of the Mappa Mundi survived, although one corner
had been chewed by mice before the picture
was made – already, the fragment of the world
containing Hamburg had been lost.

2

The Map of the Angels

Poor broken world, no way to dream
you whole again, and yet it is good to sleep
under this giant mandala: part vision,
part world that we know, it rises each night
above our bed. Mornings we set out to explore,
and gradually I start drawing for myself
a map of places angels have appeared. Mother,
while you push a little further each day in Indiana,
I'm marking the locations where things
that never happened once took place: look, here
on Waldemarstraße, so close to our flat, the exact
spot an angel gave up immortality to become human.

~

We follow a friend's directions
to Theodor-Wolff-Park, the place where the angel
fell in love with a girl who could fly on trapeze.
An old man there talks loudly to himself in Turkish
(or maybe he's setting the invisible angels straight).
That afternoon, we search in vain for the place
where Peter Falk, waiting for his scene, asked
an old woman if he could draw her.
I put Falk on the border of my map, sketching
a portrait of a woman who has a star of David
stitched on her coat. *Extras*, Falk thinks,
these humans are extras, extra humans?

~

Next on my map, Potsdamer Platz, once
the busiest intersection in the world and then,

after the war, a bombed-out field, *a no man's land*
in the middle of nowhere. Eighty years earlier,
Curt Bois was a child when he acted in his first film.
In *Wings of Desire* he is Homer, a man searching
for the city he once knew, but finding nothing
except an old couch in the wasteland by the Wall.
Now, even the Wall is gone, replaced by vendors
who sell glossy maps to supplement
my own crude one, directions for pilgrims
who miss their old belief in angels.

~

Bois died soon after the Wim Wenders film
was made, and my mother is gone now, too – but no,
in the poem it is still March, I get to tell her
about finding so many places that never existed,
and how the trees in Kreuzberg ache
for just a few warm days to burst forth. And she tells me
how she wants to see the relatives this summer.
A loud plane, low above the city. Bruno Ganz says
sometimes, when he's flying, a woman will recognize
him – it's always a woman – and say something like
Look, an angel! We don't have to worry.
And the strangest part is, she'll mean it.

~

The graffiti above our corner grocery reads, *This*
is not America. Here is not everywhere. One must
choose between worlds, so Mother asks *Why Berlin?*
and I go on my walkabout, almost unforgivably
happy, take my cheap reading glasses from my pocket
every few blocks, bend them back into shape
though I've moulded them so many times who knows
what they should look like. I put a new detail

on my map, though no map tells me anything about where she is now. I stand on the street corner, lost and not lost, collecting stories to tell her when I next call, studying the way things go in this world.

Notes from the Night Shift

Alice Minot Deppe, 1924–2009

The Other Side of First Street

Driving at dusk to the hospital to sit up
with my mother, I paused at the crossroads
where half a century ago, as I walked home
from school, a cloudburst
fell on the street's far side while sun
kept shining on mine. The storm stood still,
the stern crossing guard laughed
as she escorted us back and forth
to the rain's verge, and even the drivers
of the cars she'd stopped got out to watch.
And some of us put out our hands to touch
the rain, and some of us stepped in
and came out again, so all these years later,
stopping at this intersection en route
to the hospital, I imagine stepping
back and forth between worlds until morning.

18 April 2009

No, I seemed rooted on this side, but while
I sat by Mother, telling her about the flight
from Ireland, she suddenly gasped,
the violent rising of her ribs dislodged my hand
from her shoulder, and she stopped breathing,
ten seconds, twenty, so I knew.
Then she sipped air again, my brother
swabbed her mouth, and her breathing became steady
as a swimmer's. But when I checked her pupils,
they no longer reacted to light. Something had left
and something had not. All night, that unchanging
respiration, and I pictured her strong crawl
carrying her past the islands of her childhood,
past Naushon and Nashawena, past Cuttyhunk
with its red-winged blackbird songs
at the edge of the world.

Monitoring Nightmares

On the third night, I watched runs
of ventricular tachycardia glide past
on her monitor, signatures with billowing sails
interrupting her regular rhythm. When I worked
as a night nurse, those large-winged arrhythmias
used to visit my nightmares: any moment,
the heart could end things. She kept swimming.
Towards morning, I searched on my laptop
for my 1990 journal, wanting details of the cruise
to Cuttyhunk with my parents.
Mother was never more at home than on a boat,
or in water. I clicked on the icon for that journal,
but there was an error, the file could not be retrieved.
1990 was the first year to vanish.

Swimming Out Further

That afternoon, the phone rang. Annie said:
Your mother is dying. I wanted to dress,
have her pick me up, but she said, *It's happening,*
now. I asked her to get off the phone,
be with my mother. Later, she described
those moments so vividly
that if I don't write this down – her telling me
all this, me seeing it as she speaks – if I don't
somehow fix my absence, some future me
will believe I was in the room myself,
not five miles away standing naked by the bed,
thanking my mother, talking to her
in the middle of a blinding cloud.

Mother, while I slept at home, Doug
sang to you, a song he'd made up, an unrecorded,
unwritten, irretrievable song.
I would like to have heard the youngest son
sing to his mother. Then Annie and Joan saw
what I had seen, that you were swimming,
steady little breaths until your lips paused,
and everyone leaned forward until Dad said,
Get a nurse! and Annie and Joan said, *No. Don't.*

Breathing

The next night, unable to sleep,
I listened to distant trains,
then got up for whiskey and heard my father
breathing in his bedroom. And I found myself
timing his breaths, the way I'd timed hers.
My earliest memory: she held me at the roundhouse
in Superior as engines entered the station, turned,
re-emerged. Strange not to have a clue where she is,
even *if* she is –
          Mother of doubts as well as faith,
          Mother of questions,
          Mother of grace in the midst of uncertainty.

Michael

Our youngest son woke from a dream
in which my mother hugged him
at his sister's wedding. Knowing
his Granny was dead, he wondered
if others could see her, too,
or if they thought him mad, talking
to the tent's empty corner.
Mother, I'm still waiting for a visit from you,
though perhaps I'm too stunned for it yet.
Or maybe it's you who are stunned
somehow on your own side.
Or maybe such a comfort
would only leave me more bereft.

Song

And then, after I said farewell beside the furnace,
after days of talking to her like this on paper,
which is what I seem able to do,
I found myself by chance in our old home,
the house on Maxwell Lane that I hadn't been in
for decades, and two former neighbours
and a girl who was visiting from Budapest
guided me through the home place,
though I did most of the talking.
They let me name the place of the fire,
the place where I once flew, the place
where I lay in fear until Mother led
the nightmare bear away with a jar of honey.
And when we came downstairs,
the dark-eyed girl sang in Hungarian, a song
for the kitchen of my childhood,
and I don't know what
the words meant, but I was standing
in that cloud of tears again,
everything almost too bright to see
as if the spark at the centre of each word
were visible and moving in patterns
that might be a lament for a loved one,
or for a vanished homeland,
yet somehow the glow and lift of those notes
gladdened this spring kitchen
as if all that is lost could return,
at least for the length of a song.

Midsummer, Orkney

for Kate Newmann
who first led us to the Italian Chapel
through her poem of that name

What the bookseller tells me: Live on Orkney
long enough, you'll enter a pub and see someone
who's dead. You'll recognize the voice, rejoice
in a smile or wave of hand,
then see it's kin to the one who's lost.

~

On deck the fog-ferry from Scrabster, I watched
for the Old Man of Hoy: nothing in the mist
but guillemots ghosting the North Sea. Two months
since Mother's deathbed. She's not coming back,
even in a dream.

~

Prowling low over Cuween hill in broad daylight,
a short-eared owl inscribes a widdershins circle
around us. Each evening we see more.
Summer nights on Orkney are too short for hunting;
owls have no choice but to appear in the lit world.

~

On Lamb Holm, from scrap iron, from scavenged
wood of a wrecked ship, from memory and longing,
Italian prisoners transformed two Nissen huts
into a church. A vision that was incomplete
at war's end, so Chiocchetti refused to leave.

~

And, if my mother cannot or will not reappear,
does that mean things are complete?
After World War II, universities used huts like these
for student housing. My father laughs
when I tell him, but I always thought our first house

~

was such a hut, part of a neighbourhood
of big tin cans, laid on their sides and half-buried,
each with its own postage-stamp of lawn,
each with its single tree –
unsightly, yet somehow home.

~

That *somehow* is this chapel's foundation.
Seen from the side, there's no disguising
the Nissen huts, but from the front the façade
is perfect, like a wedding cake from Italy's Alps.
We step through the glistening portico.

~

After all that dreaming and labour, after covering
concrete with plasterboard, after that plasterboard
was painted to resemble fine carved bricks,
after so much invention, at what point
did prison become sanctuary?

~

Sky burials. Five thousand years ago,
Orkney's dead were offered to white-tailed
sea eagles. Excarnated, the skeletons
were buried in a tomb near the cliff tops
along with a totem of talons.

~

On a sun-struck afternoon, we enter
the Tomb of the Eagles. I lie on a wheeled pallet
then pull on an overhead rope to skateboard
into the land of the dead. I cross that threshold
first, so I can stand alone in her absence.

~

There seems nothing to say
about this nothingness. But when I pull myself
out on my little chariot, it is like being blinded
by cliff light and sea pinks, like being reborn
from silence into curlew call and lark song.

~

Festival week, and all over Orkney musicians try
to raise the dead. In Saint Magnus Cathedral,
two Danes perform *Petrushka* on accordions –
Stravinsky! Mother played this once
so I could dance for her,

~

then twelve years later, waking in Italy
to find a dusting of snow on my sleeping bag,
I strode down towards the Arno
singing *Petrushka* as the sun rose
as if no other music could contain such joy.

~

When the accordions transmogrify into violins
and organs, the red sandstone church begins to lift,
and from that earthquake of chords, I think
she might appear. No, the music is the only miracle.
The great stone columns only seem to rise.

~

Seven days of song and sun, and something
heartens me – I want to say this week is timeless
as a childhood summer, except time is fully present,
time is what I step back into
as I leave each chambered grave on Orkney.

~

Cuween, Unstan, the Tomb of the Eagles,
Maeshowe – time warms my face, I stand up
straight again and see the owl circling us
and write it all down quickly: flamenco
like sudden flames in the church at Deerness,

~

Dark Island ale with my wife and friends
in Stromness, the Stones of Stenness, and the four
insouciant oystercatchers who saunter in the road
in front of our car and will not scare; and time,
that old enemy, is nothing but gift,

~

it doesn't need this little chapel I've been making
all week out of scavenged tunes and words.

Midsummer sun
holds me. For this moment, at least,
all I have to do is breathe and be.

Water from the Well

No more poems about the old family well!
Things change. We can't keep whinging
about time passing – that's what my Dublin friend

just told me on the phone, but this evening,
going out for water, I've stepped into a vision
of hedges roiling in the wind, two frenzied rows

of fuchsia against a backdrop of black clouds.
So many blossoms have already fallen
that our narrow road's a long red carpet,

an invitation to march singing through Meenala,
but because the gale blowing in
from the North Atlantic may by morning

strip this glen of the colour red, a feeling of forlorn
cheer rises in me, the distillation of everything
I've learned, a need to celebrate what I can,

carry home good cold water.
Impossible not to miss the scarlet flares
of fuchsia, but also nonsense to hold on,

which is the mournful tone of this November song,
the sort of tune Kierkegaard might have hummed
after reading Dostoyevsky, some dark satisfaction

prompting him to promise never to open another book
unless its author had first faced a firing squad.
There is no record that Dostoyevsky himself

raised a tune that Christmas night when –
shackled and shivering beside a gendarme
in an open sleigh – he set off for Siberia.

But later, writing about that moment,
he confessed to being surprised by a rush
of gratitude: the hoax of a firing squad

ended as scripted with the czar's
last-minute reprieve, and now, after eight months
in prison, he was outdoors, the sleigh

was passing the festive lights of friends' homes,
and suddenly, out of his savoured bitterness,
the possibility arose of a new and serious joy.

The Rain Becomes Part of the World

Mary Donnelly, mixed media, 38cm x 38cm

This fine fall day – hazy blue hills
and sun on the rowan tree's red berries –
she's made a marvellously bleak
painting. Vertical slashes

march above a thin green swathe, while below
darkness grows darker. A storm
brought inside. Painting as preparation
for winter in Connemara.

~

At Kylemore, floods almost reach the road,
but we continue through the rain-gashed
Inagh Valley to Galway for our neighbour's show.
Soulscapes of the valley we're travelling through.

~

Rain and wind claim power. We build a fire,
find candles, read aloud my favourite uncle's stories,
dramas from Mother's family. *It's all fiction,*
she said, then took pains showing how he'd bent

time, but with both now gone, I've only the stories.
In Maine long ago, Uncle Stephen wrote until noon
then joined us to help play host:
What lasts must come first.

~

Nothing, of course, lasts. These boglands,
nine-tenths water, must be connoisseurs
of winter storms,
and we tenants at the window,

we who are only six-tenths rain, what can we do
but mourn and be grateful? Long and by long
and longer, even the sorrow for those we've loved
rushes downstream.

An Art Critic and the Colour Yellow

She waits for the museum guard to turn away,
  readying herself to touch

the young woman who is stepping into a tub,
  weight on the foot already in the bath

while her back leg tightens to follow. Viewed
  from behind, the bather is present,

seen fully, alive in a way the aging art critic
  fears she will never be again.

Impossible man, Degas! Irascible
  as her department head

who ridiculed her latest book. And yet
  it was given to Degas

to draw well. That's what he had inscribed
  on his gravestone: *He liked*

very much to draw. Now someone's asked the guard
  a question,

the critic closes her eyes and for a few seconds
  runs her spotted hand

across the oils of a masterpiece, the way
  the elderly Degas

interrogated the paintings of Ingres. Too blind
  to work,

he'd daily made his way through Paris
  to touch

the work of his teacher. She imagines his fingers,
  almost numb, searching

for the nub where paint quickens, the farewell
  and relearning

of all we aspire to. The disciple said he felt
  the rising sweep of a colour

he could no longer see but knew must be
  Indian yellow –

he felt its flame, so the critic tries now to feel
  the yellow Degas used. Tries,

and fails. But what did she think it would be like?
  Degas, after touching

the master's paintings, said, *What a horrible thing*
  yellow is! –

sulphurous blaze that leads to the end of things,
  to the heart of things,

brief flare and snuff his fingers gratefully suffered.
  Hell, she thinks,

then let me feel the horror
  of it,

and without checking the guard, returns her palm
  to the bather's back,

closes her eyes once more, and feels instead
herself young again –

slender, risen on a hot afternoon
in the south of France

from the bed of her lover, one foot entering
cool water.

Notes from a Novelist
(*La Vie Impossible*)

1

In the doctor's office, the novelist avoids
contagious magazines on the coffee table
and unfolds instead her still unused
souvenir handkerchief from Paris,
reads Metro routes printed on cloth, imagines
a journey south from the Seine:
Odéon to Montparnasse and on to Malakoff,
a name she thinks she recalls.

And now the elderly man sitting next to her peeks
at her map, maybe travelling the Metro himself?
Something makes her think: he's old enough
to have been in wartime Paris. She doesn't disturb
his gaze, lets him take that train as far as he can
on the blue-inked lines of the underground.

2

Bed rest, antibiotics, a hot whiskey,
so she reads her Paris journal, 2007, and yes,
Christian Boltanski lives in Malakoff.
And here's the character sketch she made
after visiting his installation –
Boltanski says he turned to art
when his childhood died, which means
most days now he does nothing,

just shows up at his studio
a little before lunch
and marks time (good ideas are rare).
Still, he's got a gift
for doing nothing until something strikes him –
how to get THAT into my novel?

3

Boltanski says he sometimes dreams
he's a teacher
though he rarely goes to class,
so probably he's a poor teacher,
or maybe not lecturing students
is, in itself, the lesson?
He hangs out in Malakoff,
making the case –

the same case
she used to make herself
before the good reviews and new appointment.
The necessary case
for loafing and inviting one's soul.
For doing nothing.

4

Since her debut novel *(A natural*
writer! ... Unlimited potential!)
six springs, six false starts –
may her sabbatical year change this!
She closes her eyes to nap
and finds herself in Boltanski's installation,
but finds it almost easier to see now
than it was in Paris

where a bricolage of a life was lovingly archived
in newspaper clippings, snapshots, shadows, letters,
but everything jammed together
in poor light, one thing half buried by the next,
as if memory dims
even our most vivid moments.

5

Three glorious days in which she is too ill
to lecture, but not too sick to read –
first a book on the Apollo missions
and those footprints that no wind will rewrite.
Almost everyone born before 1969
remembers Neil Armstrong's giant step
and the little installation
we left behind on the moon.

Even those born after
1969 might remember it, the way she recalls
Delft, where her family lived for a year
before her birth: when she first visited,
she exclaimed, *Delft is still just*
as I remember it!

6

Half a billion people watched on TV,
and what she recalls are black-and-white images
seen in a pub in County Cork, in Allihies.
The locals called it American propaganda:
It's all done with trick photography!
Or maybe they liked pulling the legs
of the American girls, who kept insisting
This is really happening!

But here's the thing: last summer she found
her journal for 1969, and on 20 July she and her sister
were camping in Clare, nowhere close to Allihies.
They read Yeats to the still unconquered moon.
So where did this detailed memory come from?
When did she rewrite what really happened?

7

And then at a party last month,
she caught herself
describing Allihies again,
and remembered
this story could not be true.
And nevertheless, finished telling it.
Well, it's one thing to make up stories
one later believes –

that's what we do, like it or not,
cut and paste, layer and revise
to make some sort of meaning.
But if one knows
a story is untrue, if one persists
in telling it anyway?

8

And the time came when her son asked
if there really was a Santa.
Tell me the truth, he said,
as if he meant it.
And when she did
he seemed grateful.
But a year later,
he believed once more

in the sleigh and the saint
and the chimney,
which made a better story
than whatever truth she'd come up with
to explain those gifts that arrive
while we sleep.

9

She thought of her son
while she read Nazim Hikmet,
who recalls Ramadan night when he was eight,
and how he walked hand in hand
with his grandfather to a shadow play.
Maybe nothing like this
ever happened, Hikmet admits,
maybe I read it somewhere,

but he cherishes that evening in Istanbul
anyway, he remembers
the holiday joy rising in
lantern-lit streets
until that boy he once was
couldn't contain so much happiness.

10

Rather than pick up the germ-ridden magazines
on the waiting room table, the old man
pulls out his handkerchief and studies
the Metro's map printed on it. A souvenir
of his trip to Japan in 1990,
it's the subway system in Nagoya,
and he travels south on memory's underground,
Hibino, Tokai-Dori, Minato,

and it's 1945, his is one of hundreds
of B-29s that light up the night sky
above boiling canals –
whole neighbourhoods
of wood-and-paper homes
disappear in tidal waves of flame.

11

So now, old enough that his children
worry about him wandering alone, he travels
the rebuilt city, gets off the train in Minato,
enters a museum and finds himself
stepping through a door
onto a wooden walkway
that curves across the room
and disappears through another door.

Below him is the Lake of the Dead, piled high
with clothes – blouses, shirts and kimonos, each
on top of the other. So he thinks, as he slowly crosses
Boltanski's narrow catwalk, if he falls
he will not break a hip, the clothes will cushion him
as he drowns –

12

This is the start of the novel, she knows it:
this former bomber has told very few people about
the city in flames beneath his plane, but those
tellings crystallized into story, which, lived with
long enough, became the truth that made
making his morning coffee possible. He believes
his own story, or thinks he does, but venturing into
this installation something happens – he wavers

up there, then lowers himself to the walkway, labours
to take off his shoes and jacket, drops them
with his wallet and passport into the lake, and walks
out onto the street, which is only the beginning –
he is greeted outside by terrifying sunlight,
and the novelist has no idea where he will go next.

A Choreographer in Cordes

In Cordes, everything is beautiful, even regret.

– Albert Camus

Perfect, the sunlit pigeons. From these heights
he watches them sweep around the hill town
then fly in together to the red-tiled roof
below him, wings outstretched and riding gold light.
At his table on the terrace, the grieving
choreographer readies his camera for the moment
the flock will rise and circle Cordes-sur-Ciel,
a movement perhaps for his next dance

which he tentatively names *Regret*,
though at once he knows that's too mild
a word for the dance he imagines, something to do
with the genocide of the Cathars
who once thrived here. Camera poised, he waits
for the birds to ascend, but they now seem settled
for the night, so – when his bill is paid
and the late sun is just right – he checks

to be sure he isn't seen, then flings his fork
across the alley, where it bounces
on the roof below him. The pigeons startle
but stubbornly hold their place, and it's his old
problem, how to set things in motion. He studies
the silverware on the tables around him –
twenty dancers – pictures them prone
on the dance floor, glowering at the audience.

He makes them refuse to dance. And what
did he think, after the extermination of a people,
he could make art? Then sees, at that moment
of negation, the body of his former lover,

or what seems to be his carved and
handsome image, as on a sarcophagus, at peace.
He picks up his spoon and wants to hurl it,
then stops, closes his eyes, begins to draw.

STEVEN WIGGINS, THE HARROWING

My first two days home – no children
at the playground. They've read about my release,
or their parents have. Sorry to think
they don't dare play here.

~

A small group this morning. The tallest boy,
acting as lookout, sneaks glances
at my windows to see if I am targeting them.
As if I would shoot children.

~

Still skittish today: the lanky one looking up
at my home. I want to reassure them, want to explain
what it is to be a hunter. Better not talk to them.
Better not try and explain again to anyone.

~

More themselves now. I watched the tall kid
marking out boundaries in gravel,
then seeming to explain to the rest
the rules of some new game.

~

Watched until I understood. It's clear the chosen
child has to be Steven Wiggins.
The child who is *It* must hunt the others,
who are deer, because once in a waking dream

~

I lured deer to the park's fence with apples
then took them by bow and arrow.
Now my so-called crime has become a game.
A boy tempts other children with apples.

~

They always aim for the feet. Any child
hit by an apple must wait at the base of the tree
to be freed. Steven Wiggins calls to the others, sings
to them, and they inch forward, ready to flee.

~

A newspaper photo of one of the park's
three new deer. A young buck's rough tongue
takes apples from the hands of one of my children.
The boy who just today was Steven Wiggins.

~

Someone knocked at my door. No one there
when I answered. Sometimes I'm sure
they've been peeking through my window.
The game's rules keep changing.

~

I picture the buck massaging velvet antler nubs
on chain-link, raw horn poking up through red flesh.
I picture the tall boy pulling back
a phantom bowstring and killing it.

~

Went to Mass the first time in how long?
The words say I am forgiven. The words say
I am part of the Christ. But what I have done,
I cannot undo. It is out there. It is in the game.

~

Dreamed I was killed and waiting at the tree
to be freed. Something terrible waited in the darkness
between me and the others. I couldn't wait endlessly,
hand held out, waiting for a touch.

~

I still see the buck, crumpled
against the shed. The doe pacing slowly
with my arrow's broadside in her brain.
Like a dream in which I was wide awake.

~

I was neither drunk, nor crazy, nor hungry,
nor in any need I can name. I did this,
I have confessed this, but that does not keep
the damn thing from unfolding.

~

A knock at the door, then another, then another –
no one is running away. It is the Lord,
or the police, or the children, or the deer.
I move towards the door, ready to open.

Piano Concerto in D Major for the Left Hand

Odysseus wouldn't have had to be chained to the mast
if the sirens had only been reading from the score
– Vaughan Williams

1

We're in Paris, I think, listening to jazz
and savouring a Scottish ale called
Stars over Stromness,

and it's a good night until I mention
Ravel's *Piano Concerto for the Left Hand,*
then the composer we've been drinking with

transmogrifies
into Maurice Ravel and declares
Paul Wittgenstein was an animal! Better amputate

both hands
than to still have one and make such sounds!
Turns out we're sitting in wooden choir stalls

from the twelfth century, Ravel insists I stand
and look at the carving beneath my seat – *There!*
See the wild boar playing the organ! That

is your Paul Wittgenstein.
It was given to him only to make the music
of a wild boar!

I buy the next round,
try to guide the talk away from music,
though Ravel isn't done raving.

2

Only once, in Languedoc, have I come face to face
with a wild boar. I'd left the inn past midnight

after an argument and, striding past a garden
at the village edge, met my first *sanglier*.

I've read since that, if surprised or threatened, boars
lower their heads as they charge and then

slash upwards, while sows, tuskless, race at you
with head high, mouths wide open.

This one – male or female – retreated
into steep black mountain silence.

3

For Paul Wittgenstein, the one way to reach
his mother was music –

she seemed at ease entertaining Brahms or Mahler
but her own eight children baffled her.

Still, playing piano four-hands with her
Paul sensed a thaw (*In our family, only*

when we weren't talking did we make any sense).
So, in spite of the bullet that cost his arm,

in spite of prison, in spite of the lost war,
in spite of two brothers who had taken their lives

and made suicide a constant option, in spite of
bouts of madness and his mother's death,

in spite of Maurice Ravel himself,
Paul Wittgenstein meant to play Ravel.

This was Paris, January 1933: Wittgenstein
had commissioned the music, paid for it, it was his;

Maurice Ravel had written the concerto,
it would bear his name, it was his.

*Performers must not be slaves! One must always
interpret the music,* the pianist insisted.

*Performers are
slaves*! Ravel replied. And that

is when the boar's music began,
Ravel conducting, the orchestra on his side,

and Wittgenstein working the pedals too much,
understanding Ravel

and raging against him,
inclining his head and charging.

4

Tonight, having found a recording
of Wittgenstein playing the *Concerto*
for the Left Hand, I suspect his critics were right –

the performance shows passion and skill,
yet he sounds not quite at one
with the music, Ravel seems to elude him.

And if his playing Ravel was really about
himself, not the *Concerto,* if it was only there
to give a one-armed man a chance to dazzle,

then it never transcended that inner roar.
And yet it did, at least, help him survive.
It's as if, in that prison moment when he refused

suicide and dedicated himself to music
– *Now all the important*
decisions have been made – he willfully

closed himself off from so much else –
So be it – as he sketched a keyboard
on a crate and played Chopin,

his left fingers banging at charcoal keys,
his absent right hand ghosting
its role a while, then departing for good,

so he had to imagine one hand
making the sound of two, or maybe three or four,
why do it at all if he only sounded normal?

I think of the Languedoc garden
where I encountered that beast, the sunflowers
trampled, the earth near the rope swing uprooted,

a swing placed just far enough
from the valley's edge
that a child could glide up and safely see

all that emptiness stretched beyond.
The air near the village slaughter hall
was wet with blood

but so far this wonderful monster had escaped,
it was there to confront me.
In winter, one can watch them

on the opposite ridge,
like a moving tableau, the boar
zigzagging up the mountain,

the men and dogs in pursuit, but in summer
the forest screens the hunt, there are only the sounds
of guns and dogs and shouts.

Mother, listen,
in spite of the loss of my right hand,
in spite of war and prison,

in spite of the fact that you are no longer here,
I've made at least this music.
I've paid for it. It is mine. And I offer it to you.

Bavarian Landscape with a Yellow House

in memory of Isabel Lewando

1

Because death gets the last word,
and because this week I've thought of
little else, I'll begin with her birthplace.
Because we couldn't attend
her funeral in Maine, we rented a car in Berlin,
drove to Bavaria to say goodbye,
and there – using a photograph
of a photograph of the family home –
found the place near a village crossroad,
where a Maypole stood year-round.

2

Because the meadows in that village
were greener than Ireland,
because the apples were the largest
I've ever seen, because the sunflowers
in those gardens could light up
the underworld, and because we'd lost
our friend, we lingered
in that place of light and shadow,
and found there the same landscape
that has floated above our dreams all autumn.

3

We've slept each night in our rented flat in Berlin
under a framed print of Kandinsky, a landscape
in which clouds, hills and white dabs that might
be sheep can still be identified – it's only 1909,
the represented world hasn't wholly given way
to Kandinksy's *inner necessities*
and *spiritual relationships*.
The Garmisch-Munich train approaches a darkness
of hills or forests, or both, and before that, in a bright
green valley, there's a yellow house with a red roof.

4

Because death gets the last word but we wanted
an after-word with our friend, we drove to Bavaria
and found the house Gabriele Münter bought in 1909.
As though the years Münter and Kandinsky
spent wandering together – Dresden, Tunisia,
Berlin, Rapallo – were to find this house in Murnau
where Kandinsky painted horses on the stairs,
a rush of bright riders ascending, and Münter's
windowscapes showed how the everyday
could gather speed, could glide.

5

And was it a house that Annie and I were
searching for, too? As though this decade
on the road – Cape Clear, France, Galway, Berlin –
a decade of wandering that not having a house
made possible — was a search for a space to flourish?
Though not this house, the Münter-Haus
has already been lived in thoroughly, it is a museum
now, it is the past. But does our mutual,
unexpectedly emotional response to this home
say something about what must perhaps come next?

6

It is not enough, I know, to set rooms down
on paper. At some point, one should carve
those rooms in stone. Though of course
beneath Kandinsky's green hill
there is that nightmare I had of the terrifying
stone library where everything
one writes is archived; one can never take back
a single word; we who write, build in stone;
room upon endless room records it all,
every word another stone around our necks.

7

Because death, by right of eminent domain,
claims the ground floor, I place a studio above that
for art, and above that a room for music – make it
the concert hall on Oranienburger Straße
where we waited for the trio to begin
the night before we learned of our friend's death.
And how the young cellist that night reminded me
of a high school girlfriend who told me I should
become an architect: *It's a respectable*
way to make art! Recalling her,

8

I laughed in the concert hall, trying to reconcile
her vision of me with the years I later worked
in a hospital, and how each night I had to solve
again the maze of halls. That same
spatially-challenged part of me realized,
when the Brahms began, I would never quite
understand the best chamber music,
as phrases branched out and explored
unexpected corridors and found their way home,
delighting me in ways I could never explain.

9

We walked back to our flat, so happy, then got
the message about Isabel's death. That night
and then the next day nothing cohered.
On the second night, I found I could stream
her favourite station, WBACH Radio, which she
played for beach-goers who passed her house
in Maine. I let the music play loudly enough
to be heard on the street, hopefully not so loud
that it disturbed sleepers, and what came on
was Mendelssohn's *A Midsummer Night's Dream*.

10

Mendelssohn, whose trio was played after Brahms
last week, a piece so clear even I could see its structure
(did that disappoint me a little?), Mendelssohn,
who is buried in this Berlin neighbourhood,
and whose deathbed scene made everyone laugh
when the violinist told us how a brass band
passed under the window where Mendelssohn
lay unconscious, and how he leapt from bed as if
to conduct them, then fell back to the waiting sheets –
a good death, could one call it that, at age thirty-eight?

11

The *Midsummer Night's Dream* reached its famous
wedding march, and I recalled my youngest son's
ceremony two months earlier, and how a random
guitarist showed up on the beach and played
Pink Floyd's *Outside the Wall* as the barefoot,
radiant bride crossed the length of sand chosen as aisle,
and for a fleeting moment things connected – death,
weddings, and music were part of the one house,
and a couple passing by, hearing the wedding march,
looked up and waved, then walked in time away.

12

Two words from *Howards End* came to me, *Only*
connect, and I thought what strange afterlives
we're given, words that come to the minds of others,
asked for or not, or a phrase of song that goes out
into the world. My friend's music delighted
so many passersby that I wanted the radio host
to somehow know, to dedicate the Mendelssohn to her.
When he didn't, I leaned from the window and said
something into the Berlin night, like *Isabel Lewando,*
if you can somehow hear, these words are for you.

13

No. Words are not a place to live,
but one might make a little shrine
to mark a friend's passing.
What good, anyway, is a house when one dies?
Four walls to surround
what can no longer be contained.
And yet, while she was alive, that home in Maine
gave Isabel space to paint and write
and take photographs, it gave her a place to raise a son,
it gave them a chance to flourish.

14

Late last night, I lay down in the days of 1909
under a hill in Murnau, and though the Great War
gathered like the distant Alps, there was still time
for me to be Gabriele Münter
and paint two Russian friends
reclining before a single Bavarian peak.
Then I was Kandinsky, dreaming of forsaking
the *seen* so I could free myself to wander
the realm of the spirit, though it was 1909
and I still had one foot in the visible.

15

Then I was Isabel Lewando.
I opened the window
and played WBACH Radio for passersby –
is this all there is to our afterlives?
Surely there is something more?
From that antechamber of a dream, I climbed
from bed with what seemed the right words to begin
this piece: *Since death is part of it all,*
and never therefore nothing, it's the ground floor,
the place from which to start building.

December Evening, Berlin

What's wrong? she asks as his face scrunches up
as though realizing something terrible,

but he'd just been recalling
what he'd heard on his walk, the sound

of flapping wings moments before the snow began,
and how he'd looked up and –

briefly misplacing continents – thought
Canada geese, no, *swans*,

then followed their flight above the canal,
their silence saying something

beyond speech. It was the not-saying-anything
of the swans that he was trying to understand,

and, when he sees her trying to read his face,
for a moment he has no words.

Later, going to bed, he remembers her question
and the wordless place he'd been

where silence seemed to have nothing to do
with nothingness

but was the force that drove the thumping wings,
and turning to her, he says, *Everything's alright,*

and below them is the city
of canals and rivers and light.

COMING HOME TO THE NORTH COUNTRY

First the night train, then the long drive
to Superior for an overdue visit to the past.
In an hour, the temperature fell fifty degrees,
so no surprise that my first home,
reappearing after six decades,
did so beneath hail, beneath lightning.
Then further back, crossing
the bridge to Duluth –
June, but balls of ice on the roadside
like welcoming confetti.
We found St Luke's, took the elevator
to the birthing centre above the stormy
and shimmering lake. Impossible to go
further back in this world. From the ground
of things, a sudden bright tremor.

~

I knew that Bobby Zimmerman and I
first drew breath in the same hospital,
but I hadn't realized until now
that I was born on Desolation Row.
Once, I might have said that
with a sort of pride,
or played it for the joke,
but I just learned that eight blocks
and thirty years from my birth
our townspeople lynched
three black circus workers.
And yes, they sold postcards
of the hanging, violent images
you can find online, though you may not
want to. I can't stop seeing
the mutilated men. And the faces

in the crowd. Everyone mugging
for the camera. Everyone smiling
on cue for the hangman.

~

We drove north on old Highway 61 to spend
the night in a lighthouse. Deer in the garden,
otter by the shore, and my wife invited me
to a sunset walk on the breakwater.
Halfway, fog barrelled in, lightning
in the distance, and the couple in front
turned back. First, a gleaming wedge
of reddish grey erased the jetty's end. Then
we were in it, too, out of sight of land, claimed
by the marvellous. Deep horn
of an ore freighter, faraway thunder, waves
breaking beneath us, and the narrow, wet jetty
made me question going on, but my wife
quoted Dickinson: *If your Nerve, deny you –*
Go above your Nerve.
No way to watch her disappear
alone, so, reciting my given lines,
I followed. Then we stepped through
the cloud curtain – we were out at the end,
everything red-gold and impossibly clear,
and the storm
already a fold in the past's long veil.

~

Arriving too late for anyone to greet us,
we found instructions
signed by *The Lighthouse Ghost.*
One note invited us
to a slice of rhubarb pie. The next warned us

not to play the gramophone. My wife
wound the crank, placed the needle
onto an old 78, and was rewarded
by 'West End Blues'. The lighthouse,
the music, the furnishings,
all stepped from another era. Was the ghost
watching us disobey? Or did she forget us
after the piano solo, as I forgot almost everything
and concentrated on Louis Armstrong's
one held trumpet note
that hovered in the air with no plans
of ever coming down. It took me six decades
to revisit Highway 61, the long Blues road
that stretches from New Orleans
to the North Country. A sustained note
that follows the Mississippi most of the way,
past the spot where Bessie Smith died,
past the crossroads where Robert Johnson
bargained with the devil, past the square in Duluth
of the three slain circus workers.
As if a man could put everything
he'd loved or lost into one glistening note,
make it cut through time
like a bridge we might walk back and forth on –
a way perhaps to go back even further –
and then gently, safely,
bring all that heartbreak and joy
back down to earth. When the stylus
reached the end of the record's
spiral universe, it orbited the last groove
like a glittering probe turned into space debris.
Lifting it, I moved the little diamond
back to the beginning. Crossed
the forbidden bridge one more time.

Castle Cottage

After striking my head on the lintel
of what will be my study,
not once but twice as we moved in –

After rising from the floor and wondering
would I learn such a clear lesson
quickly enough or inflict some greater damage –

After setting up the computer
in my dangerous new workroom
I typed in the search phrase,

You can't get killed
bumping your head on a lintel,
can you? And read of Charles VIII,

Charles the Affable,
who – in his magnificent chateau on the Loire –
bumped his diademed head

and, surrounded by royal guards, felled
himself. Felled, from *fellan*, Old English for fall,
related to the Old Norse for downfall, or sin,

(derived, I'm guessing,
from the Postlapsarian word for The Fall,
the lapse of man into self-consciousness).

Strange to realize I'm not sure what
consciousness is – looking it up, I find the word
first used in the sixteenth century,

meaning *to be aware of wrongdoing,*
from the Latin, *conscius,*
for *knowing with others or in oneself.*

As if language was one great circling swoon
and what we most know, with others
and in our deepest selves, is our wrongdoing,

and The Fall. No. But earlier this evening,
I took a break with Annie from unpacking.
We walked past Grace O'Malley's ruined castle,

then out to the sea cliffs, and as islands and sky
glowed in wild last light, she said, *I wasn't sure*
I'd make it. I thought she meant the move,

but she was referring to last March and her
concussion, that fierce light show inside
and the nerve storm up and down her arms

before head and neck pain went central.
Now, in my study, looking back
at looking down at waves pounding our shores,

I consider consciousness. As to this *knowing*
with others and in oneself, one thing we
know together now is the coup and contrecoup

of concussion.
Four decades since I was robbed
in Prague's main train station,

an experience that left me humiliated and furious,
but then came a surge of irrational joy –
I was twenty, I was in the most beautiful

of cities, and my inner Zorba was suddenly certain
that, following this catastrophe, something
wonderful was about to happen. And woke

in a hospital, held down by orderlies. No idea
how I'd come there, so I threw a punch, raced
for the door and was tackled – darkness again –

then woke as a gentle, blond nurse told me
Sie hatten einen Unfall –
she spoke German, I'd had an *Unfall*, an accident,

and to one so lovely I was willing to listen.
A gale has blown in, the Good Ship Castle
is riding it out so far, and it's almost midnight,

time for bed after the long move,
but I want to create, while I can,
some survival plan for life among low doors.

No more blows to the head! Which makes me hope
I didn't hurt the orderlies who tried to help me.
And who else came to my assistance? Someone

must have knelt beside me outside the station,
someone got me to the hospital, people treated me
for days and I was charged nothing (when I asked

how to pay, my baffled nurse
replied, *This is Czechoslovakia. Who would charge
you for the right of health care?*)

Ein Unfall. Felled. Fallen.
Oh, this much seems dizzily clear:
in ourselves and with others,

we are in this together.
Best perhaps lower your forehead
entering any room. Climbing into bed,

the Czech word for *thank you*
comes back from decades. *Děkuji.*
Until sleepfall, I'll try to make the word my mantra.

HOUSE NEXT DOOR TO THE END OF THE WORLD

Introitus

In the dream, I'm spreading a roll of paper
on a table, using a book spine as straight-edge
to draw lines and make staves. Composing.

Unable to read or write music, yet confident
I have everything I need to draft a Requiem Mass –
grief, hope, each possible note.

Only lacking the right architecture, the right
contours, but those are all around me
in the hills and islands of Connemara.

Offertorium

Surely this has something to do
with our friend's death,
something to do with playing Fauré

on our way back from the wake, something
to do with summer's window
being left open, so all night at the foot of our bed

there was the wash of the sea on the shingle,
that untranslatable ur-sound
that we've rented this house all year to hear.

Sanctus

Joe Kane said of Falcarragh's Backstrand
it is *the only beach*
with grain-to-grain redemption.

Once, walking that strand, as storm clouds
gathered over Horn Head, he quoted
Roethke to me. *I am that final thing, a man*

learning how to sing.
So now, five hours south, I walk
to the end of our strand, wishing my waking self

could compose music.
Get no further than finding one right note
which I give to the wind to howl.

Pie Jesu

I am falling in love with the tourists
who stay next door
at The End of the World B&B.

Arriving on this peninsula, each new guest
steps excitedly from their car, snaps
the same photos: ruined castle, unruly islands,

cloud-shadowed mountains, path to the open sea.
I'm listening to Fauré when today's couple
emerges from the guesthouse.

Standing in the frenzied foreground
as the treble solo
pleads for their eternal rest,

they look vital, filled with wonder.
I'll leave it to my dream self to compose
A Requiem for the Dearest Strangers.

Agnus Dei

I would dedicate the Requiem I cannot write
to Joe, but he didn't want a Funeral Mass.
What he said he lived for was *the true*

catholic and apostolic
house of the imagination.
Yes, it was also home to so much pain,

but having posited a roofline above his head,
having dreamed up a hallway
linking room to room,

having found, it seems,
the right architecture,
he learned at last how to sing there.

Libera me

Annie's amusement that I was composing.
But why a Requiem Mass?
Then all over again she remembers.

Fauré, agnostic, said he wrote his Requiem
simply for the pleasure.
Imagined the last sound he would ever hear,

then proposed the existence of music
beyond the grave's gate, voices that could play out
whatever happens to consciousness and love.

In Paradisum

Years ago, Joe dedicated a poem to us,
which ended with lines about the sea's *ever-*
changing conversation, a discussion

that continues through our open window
as wind and waves talk with Gabriel Fauré
about last things. And now, before leaving

the peninsula, it seems my couple is returning
from one final walk, speaking
animatedly together though I can't hear a word.

A squall crosses the water from Achill,
they may or may not make it before the rain,
but no hint of hurry. Oh most dear

strangers who live within this music,
what is it that we love so much about this view
from the edge? You linger, as if to take in further

the sea-and-rainscape, and then one of you
points to something
as the sopranos begin, *Jerusalem, Je-ru-sa-lem.*

Climbing now into your rental car
as wind and lashing rain arrive together
and purple loosestrife whips about,

you shelter in the front seat, let the wind
buffet you. Now the singers hold the last syllable.
And now, so gently, they hold the silence.

SISYPHUS

All of us carrying one thing or the other
  uphill each day,
but once the dog we called Sisyphus refused
  to climb the hill again. Sisyphus,
who followed his sociable nose downhill
  on his daily rounds,
who was part of the scene at the pier
  or shop
or the little green shoebox of The Library
  of Good Welcome,

Sisyphus, who found one evening his stiff
  and swollen joints
wouldn't let him trudge back home so he sat
  at the foot of the hill and waited.
Someone stopped and drove him up
  the Leacha Mhór.
After that he'd be there each evening, and raising
  his paw like a hitchhiker
was a formality, since everyone stopped
  anyway.

Towards the end, they'd even hoist him up
  into the car,
and then, at the gate of his home, lift him
  gently down.
All of us, carrying one thing or the other, uphill,
  as long as we're able,
which isn't forever, whatever our myths say.
  All of us,
setting off on our daily rounds, in need
  of the next welcome.

About the Author

Theodore Deppe is the author of *Children of the Air* and *The Wanderer King* (Alice James Books, 1990 and 1996); *Cape Clear: New and Selected Poems* (Salmon, 2002); and *Orpheus on the Red Line* (Tupelo, 2009).

He holds a Masters Degree in Fine Arts in Poetry from Vermont College. A recipient of two grants from the National Endowment for the Arts and a Pushcart Prize, he has been writer-in-residence at the James Merrill House in Stonington, Connecticut, and Phillips Academy in Andover, Massachusetts.

Ted has taught creative writing in graduate programmes in the US, Ireland and England. He is on the faculty of the Stonecoast Masters in Fine Arts Programme, and he directs Stonecoast in Ireland, which brings Master's degree students in Maine to study in Ireland.

He worked as a registered nurse for twenty years while teaching poetry and fiction classes. Since 2000, he and his wife, poet Annie Deppe, have, for the most part, made their home on the west coast of Ireland, and they presently live in Connemara. In 2006, he became a dual citizen of the US and Ireland.